George Whitefield CHADWICK

TAM O'SHANTER
Symphonic Ballad
(1915)

Study Score
Partitur

PETRUCCI LIBRARY PRESS

The lines of the poem "Tam O'Shanter," by Robert Burns, which have suggested this symphonic ballade, are as follows:
"The wind blew as 't were blawn its last
The rattling showers rose on the blast," etc.
[*Allegro moderato* (2/4) G minor]
A short and stormy introduction for the full orchestra leads directly to the "Tam O'Shanter" theme,
"Ae market night
Tam had got planted unco right,
Wi' reaming swats that drank divinely;"
[*Allegro comodo* (2/4) C major]
it is a jocund, roistering chorus in the style of a Scottish folk-tune, given to the horns and trombones, sometimes in different keys simultaneously, and immediately repeated by the strings and wind. This is interrupted by another burst of the storm, which shortly dies away in a roll of distant thunder.

Then begins Tam's homeward journey through the storm,
"Weel mounted on his gray mare Meg
Tam skelpit on thro' dub and mire," etc.
[*Moderato* (2/4) A minor]
a persistent trotting figure in the basses and 'cellos, with which short fragments of the "Tam O'Shanter" theme are heard in the wind instruments. This leads to a choral theme given to the trombones,
"Kirk Alloway is drawing nigh,"
[*Allegro moderato* (2/4) B♭ minor]
for which a part of the old Scottish tune called "Martyrs" has been utilized. After a climax, this comes to a sudden stop as Tam catches his first glimpse of the revels in the church. This orgy is described in a series of dances very much in the Scottish style.
"He screwed the pipes and gart them skirl."
[*Molto moderato* (2/4) D minor]
There is squealing of bagpipes (oboe and bassoon) and a rough hornpipe dance tune, "No cotillion brent new frae France" (solo viola); both tunes afterwards repeated in combination by the whole orchestra. There are rattling of bones (xylophone), unearthly shrieks from the clarinets and muted horns and dismal groans from the trombones and tuba. The tempo continually accelerates, and finally ends with a furious reel in which every instrument in the orchestra plays its loudest and fastest. Then Tam interrupts with his flattering comment, a little recitative for the horns and bassoons,
"'Weel done, cutty sark.'
And in an instant all was dark."
[*Lento*]
A moment of silence, and after two menacing notes from the gong
"Out the hellish legion sallied."
[*Allegro con fuoco-stringendo-presto-prestissimo*]
A reiterated galloping figure in the strings, accentuated by the percussion, leads the wild chase of the witches. With an awful shriek the bridge is crossed:
"Ae spring brought off her master hale
But left behind her ain gray tail."

Then follows a short interlude of plaintive character, possibly suggestive of Maggie's varied emotions. The music now loses its delineative and programmatic character, and becomes more subjective.

In the rather extended close, which is altogether reflective rather than illustrative, the "Tam O'Shanter" theme gradually returns; at first in fragments of the melody given to the wind instruments, and finally for divided strings and harp.

But here it no longer depicts the carousals of the drunken Highlanders. It is transformed into a quiet sustained melody with simple harmonizing, purely lyrical in expression. A short episode then brings back fragments of the bagpipe and fiddle dance tunes in combination with the "Kirk Alloway" chorale, suggesting perhaps the moral of the last verse of the poem,
"Remember Tam O'Shanter's mare."

The piece ends very quietly with a reminiscence of the "Tam O'Shanter" theme.

TAM O'SHANTER
SYMPHONIC BALLADE FOR ORCHESTRA BY
George Whitfield Chadwick

BOSTON : THE BOSTON MUSIC COMPANY

(facsimile of the original 1917 title page)

ORCHESTRA

3 Flutes
(3rd also Piccolo)
2 Oboes
English horn
3 Clarinets
(2 in B-flat, 1 in D)
Bass Clarinet
2 Bassoons

4 Horns
3 Trumpets
3 Trombones
Tuba

Timpani
Percussion
(bass drum, cymbals, tam tam, wooden drum, chinese drum,
sand-block, rattle, xylophone, bells)
Harp

Violins I
Violins II
Violas
Violoncellos
Double Basses

Duration: ca. 20 minutes

First performance:
June 3, 1915, Norfolk, Connecticut
Litchfield Festival Orchestra / Composer

ISMN: 979-0-58021-016-6
ISBN: 978-1-932419-09-2
This score is a slightly modified unabridged reprint of the score
issued in 1917 by Boston Music Co., Boston, plate B.M. Co. 5468.
The score has been scaled to fit the present format.

Printed in the USA
First Printing: March, 2016

To my friend, Horatio Parker

Tam O'Shanter

GEORGE W. CHADWICK

14

16

24

28

34

38

42

44

46

47

54

56

61

64

65

66

78

82

19092

94

Milton Keynes UK
Ingram Content Group UK Ltd.
UKHW051823250224
438391UK00003B/73